MW01539650

Blossom Shading Vol. 2

GRAYSCALE PHOTO COLORING BOOK FOR ADULTS

Majestic COLORING

Copyright © 2016 Majestic Coloring

www.MajesticColoring.com

All rights reserved. No part of this book may be reproduced or transmitted in any form or by any means, including but not limited to information storage and retrieval systems, electronic, mechanical, photocopy, recording, etc. without written permission from the copyright holder.

Images used under license from Shutterstock.com

ISBN: 978-1530509645

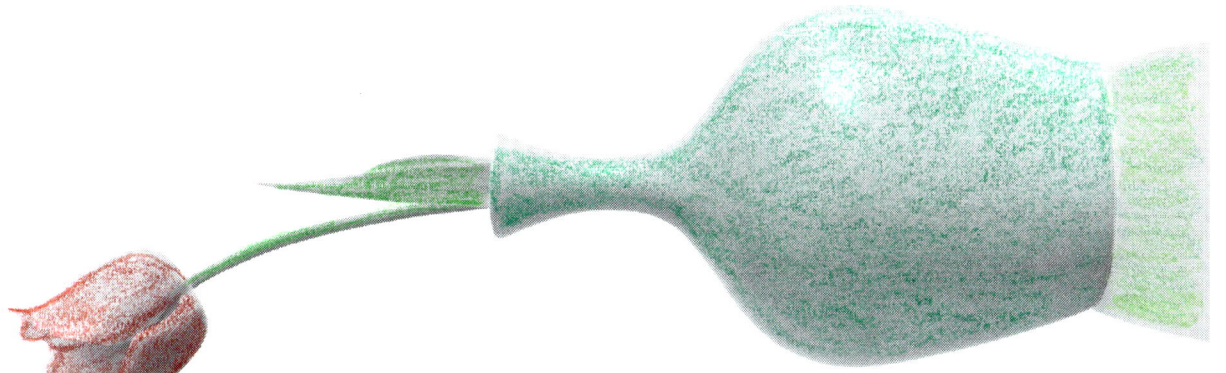

FREE DOWNLOAD

12 FUN DESIGNS FOR YOUR COLORING ENJOYMENT!

This 'n That Coloring Book for Grown-Ups is bundled up in one convenient PDF file to download and print at your leisure.

Sign up for our Majestic Coloring mailing list and get a free copy of **This 'n That Coloring Book for Grown-Ups**.

Click here to get started
http://majesticcoloring.com/thisnthat-free

39980246R00031

Made in the USA
San Bernardino, CA
08 October 2016